A
DRAGON
WALKS
INTO A BAR

300+ One-Liners, Zingers, and Jokes That Will SLAY

JEF ALDRICH & JON TAYLOR

Adams Media

New York London Toronto Sydney New Delhi

Adams Media
An Imprint of Simon & Schuster, Inc.
100 Technology Center Drive
Stoughton, MA 02072

First Adams Media hardcover edition December 2019

ADAMS MEDIA and colophon are trademarks of Simon & Schuster.

For information about special discounts for bulk purchases, please contact Simon & Schuster Special Sales at 1-866-506-1949 or business@simonandschuster.com.

The Simon & Schuster Speakers Bureau can bring authors to your live event. For more information or to book an event contact the Simon & Schuster Speakers Bureau at 1-866-248-3049 or visit our website at www.simonspeakers.com.

Interior design by Julia Jacintho and Nicola DosSantos
Interior images by Kurt Dolber; © Simon & Schuster, Inc.
Sword joke divider image © 123RF/Sergey Leonov

Manufactured in the United States of America

2 2021

Library of Congress Cataloging-in-Publication Data has been applied for.

ISBN 978-1-5072-1218-9
ISBN 978-1-5072-1219-6 (ebook)

INTRODUCTION

Why can't zombies write good music?
They can only de-compose.

Where do people buy their giant hammers?
A maul.

What's a dwarf's favorite thing to listen to?
Rock music.

Do you like to groan at awful puns? Do you enjoy clever wordplay? If you do, hail and well met! Welcome to *A Dragon Walks Into a Bar*, the only joke book for those of us who prefer to spend our time rolling dice and thinking up fantastic stuff. We didn't really do a ton of research for this thing. (All right, let's be honest: We didn't do any.) What we did do is cram this book full of the best/worst jokes we could think of so you can entertain and annoy your fellow players.

Not only did we include a selection of jokes, puns, and one-liners; we also made up some tables so you can do everything from generate random non-player characters you can use in your game

("You're greeted by an uncomfortably grimy used-cart salesman") to frightening cheese monsters ("Look! It's a group of wandering Muenstrels!"). As you read through this book, you'll need an assortment of gaming dice from the humble d6 to a d10. (There are some tables that call for rolling a number between 1 and 100, but don't panic. Just use two d10s and you're good.) Each table tells you what you'll need. We're sure you've already got plenty of dice lying around or a dice-rolling app if you're more digitally minded. At the very least, you know a friend who has far more dice than is necessary.

There's a grand total of 335 jokes, 17 tables, and 117 sidebars containing snide commentary and further information about the jokes. Dang! That's a lot of humor.

"But will this help me play my favorite RPG?" you ask. We totally and completely guarantee it will not do anything of the sort. What it will do is give you a chance to be the life of your gaming group— cracking jokes as your party runs away from a menacing blue alien with a disintegrator gun or a gang of orcs. At times like that, you all need a good snicker.

You can keep these jokes on hand for when something relevant pops up in your game, or share your favorites with the group as you find them. Or just keep them all to yourself! Who are we to say how you use this? Maybe you want to giggle quietly to yourself while reading. When your friends ask you, "What's so funny?" you reply, "Oh, nothing." But it wasn't nothing; it was this book. The important thing is that you get a good time out of it.

So sit back, put on your favorite selection of ye olde tymey gaming music, don your robe and wizard hat, and get ready to laugh. No humor checks required.

WHAT IS AN RPG?

Obviously, if you're buying a book of RPG jokes, you have the same question as anyone who's ever purchased an RPG: What the heck is this thing? Well, luckily, we're here to elucidate in a series of simple, easy-to-grasp questions and answers.

What Is an RPG?

An RPG is a special feeling. Like a tickle on the tummy from a trusted friend or the feeling you get when you find out that a horse likes you. It's like playing a board game, except you and your friends are the pieces! (You're the shoe.) Since time immemorial, humans have been playing pretend using storytellers, actors, and our own wild imagination. An RPG is like when you played cops and robbers as a kid, but with a strict set of guidelines and rules about what you can and can't do, including an arbiter who doesn't so much play the game with you as make sure you aren't playing pretend incorrectly.

What Do I Need to Play an RPG?

The tools of the trade couldn't be simpler. You'll just need an RPG (by the way, if you haven't got an RPG, get one...this isn't one...we don't know how to write RPGs), some paper, the correct dice, pencils, and some pizza certainly couldn't hurt! (Regarding dice: The important criteria in die selection are as follows: size, faces, weight, clarity, balance, color, make, density, glow, and cost. The most coveted of these is the illustrious Princess Dice.) You'll also need a place to play, like your grandparents' weird quiet house or the manga section of a bookstore. Finally, you'll need some friends who are free for several hours in a row at the same time every week. So, if you're an adult, sorry for wasting your time.

Are RPGs an Arcane Connection to Satanic Powers and Rituals?
Yeah, probably.

How Do I Do This?
Oh, it's fairly simple. Once you've generated a character using a variety of systems, you'll inhabit the mind space of that character. You don't exactly become the character, but you know a lot about her or him. And vice versa. Your character'll know your bank codes. They'll be able to say things. To your kids. But in return, you get to go on fun adventures to a dungeon! You'll get to speak in the language of yon elderre tymes! Forsooth! You'll swing swords at monsters, innkeepers, shopkeepers, and randomly encountered minstrels! It's truly the best life has to offer.

> ### ♟ JEF'S ANNOYING SIDEBARS
> When I was done writing the jokes in this book, I asked Jef to look them over. Not only did he do that; he insisted on sticking in a bunch of snarky commentary on them in the form of sidebars. If you find them as annoying as I do, just remember—it's not my fault!
> —Jon

What's the leading cause of death among RPG characters?

RPG players.

How do you make sure your players get to the adventure in the south?

Tell them they can go east, west, or north.

Did you hear about the wizard who grew one size category and then shrank five?

He was living Large for a while, but now... well, now he's just Fine, I guess.

> ### 🧙 CONCERNING SIZE CATEGORIES
> You're expecting a lot here if you think readers will want jokes that not only reference the size category system but also require them to do multiple mathematics steps.

What's the most difficult obstacle a player can face?

Scheduling a game.

Did you hear about the game master who was eating chocolate while playing?

She was accused of fudging the dice.

Does a ranger have a high nature skill?

Does a bear poop in the woods?
Well, according to a ranger, yes.

🐾 BEAR LORE

Lower nature skill scores have historically presented weird obstacles to bear knowledge for rangers or others. Low scores and rolls often lead to confused adventurers complaining that something indeterminate but honey-scented is gnawing their leg.

What happened when someone hotboxed the gaming group?

It was a total party chill.

Who was the hardest *Saved by the Bell* character to hit?

AC Slater.

> 🎩 **CONCERNING THE DANGERS OF BAYSIDE HIGH SCHOOL DENIZENS**
> AC Slater is indeed a tricky foe to hit, but I would caution wise adventurers to keep a weather eye out for the wandering Screech. While easy to hit, this fiend will immediately alert all other students in its range to danger. Additionally, it's easily, easily the worst character.

What's the most important
attribute in a player?

Free time.

How did the munchkin get into RPGs?

He met-a-game.

How is a chunky peanut butter and
marshmallow sandwich like a great RPG?

It's got the perfect balance of
crunch and fluff.

How did the rules lawyer like his vegetables?

RAW.

How did the hit point get
where it was going?

It was derived.

How can you tell a dwarf doesn't
care about something?

He doesn't mine.

What's a dwarf's favorite thing to listen to?

Rock music.

🔔 DWARVES AND MUSIC

There is no specific type of music that dwarves enjoy. Much like humans, dwarven preferences are based entirely on personal choice. That said, and I don't mind saying this, dwarf music sounds like cats being strangled by machines designed for anything besides cat strangling.

Roll for Initiative:
Roll 1d6 and fill in the blanks.

A _____ _____
[member of a villainous race]   [type of woman of the night]

walks into _____ .
[a tavern, inn, or public house]

A _____
[valorous and noble adventurer, pure of heart]

inquires as to the price of her services to the chorus of sniggers and catcalls from his companions, and, after a moment's thought, the _____ replies
[woman of the night]

"_____ ."
[witty rejoinder or clever turn of phrase]

Die Roll	Villainous Race	Type of Woman	Place	Adventurer	Witty Phrase
1	Orc	Slattern	The Pig and Whistle	Gnomish rogue	"Sex work is a respectable profession. You're on the wrong side of history, here."
2	Gnoll	Doxy	The Frog and Toad	Doughty human cleric clad in sackcloth and tonsured	"'Twould cost you but a handful of filthy coinage but would inflict no stain on your already blackened hand."
3	Bugbear	Scarlet woman	The Pork and Pie	Mysterious wizard, known to his peers as Winklefurth the Evoker	"History will vindicate my people against the naked aggression of you humans and nonhumans!"
4	Werewolf	Madame	The Rocks and More Rocks	The town fool, elevated in stature by ale and overconfidence	"RAWR!" (It turns out she only speaks the guttural language of her people and their fiendish demon cohorts.)
5	Mind Flayer	Strumpet	The Hand and Jobber	A dwarf, deep in his cups and singing loudly and off-key of the victories of his ancestors	"Come play *Evony*, my lord."
6	Catoblepas	Harlot	The Sheep, Goat, Duck, Chandler, His Wife, and Their Daughter	Carl Weathers	"Fifty bucks, same as in town."

What spell do you cast to make friends with a squirrel?

Leomund's Tiny Nut.

> 🧙 **THE TINY NUT SPELL**
> It seems as though Find Familiar would be more efficacious in this regard. That said, I have met Leomund, and his Tiny Nuts are above reproach.

What happened when the monk beat up all the archers?

There was a flurry of bows.

What's the bestselling
genre of book in the forest?

Elf-help books.

What do you call blessed metal that is mined by tiny holy people?

Faith gnome ore.

> 🧙 **CONCERNING GNOMISH MINING AND MUSIC**
> Ooh, that's a hard ore to find. Usually when you dig for it you just keep running into Mudvaynes.

Nobody trusts a bard because they're always seen walking around with a lyre.

Why did the dwarf keep hitting his party
members' belongings with a pickaxe?

Because he couldn't tell the difference
between yours and mine.

Why did Tasha need a nanny?

She had an Uncontrollable Hideous Daughter.

What's a monk's favorite drink?

You would think it's punch,
but generally it's a mild green tea.

What's the best spell for when you're hungry?

Drawmij's Instant Noodles.

> **🧙 CONCERNING MAGICAL FOOD**
> Are you quite certain? Really quite certain? With the prevalence of spells that are simply titled things such as "Create Food and Water" and "Heroes' Feast" you've decided on summoning a cup of flash-fried ramen noodles? What are you, in college?

What was wrong with Tasha's barn?

She had an Uncontrollable Hideous Rafter.

How do you make Evard laugh?

With ten-tickles.

What competition do wizards
always excel at?

A spell-ing bee.

Why do mages always prefer mithral robes?

Because they can't-rip.

🧙 WIZARDS AND THEIR ROBES
Other popular wizard robe fibers include rayon, if they're into the
direct damage stuff, or voile (don't look at me; I think they think
it's pronounced like "voila").

Roll for Initiative:

Roll percentile and fill in the blank.

_____?

[creature]

I hardly know her!

> **♟ HOW TO ROLL PERCENTILE**
> To roll percentile, take two 10-sided dice and nominate one the "tens" die. Roll them both and treat the result as a percentage. For example, if you roll a 3 on your "tens" die and a 5 on the other, you have generated 35 percent. Traditionally, rolls of paired zeroes indicate a roll of 100, not a roll of 0!

Dice Roll	Creature
1–6	Beholder
7–11	Piercer
12–13	Lurker
14–22	Cloaker
23–30	Ethereal filcher
31–32	Choker
33–41	Carrion crawler
42–50	Rust monster
51–54	Ixitxachitl
55–61	1d3 wandering minstrels
62–69	Ogre
70–77	Gibbering mouther
78–80	Norker
81–87	Salamander
88–94	Doppelganger
95–100	Muckdweller

How do wizards pay for things?

Spell check.

How do you keep your place in a spell book?

A Magic Marker.

Why does Madonna always use Silent and Still Spells?

She's a material girl.

> **A SIDE NOTE CONCERNING MADONNA, OF ALL THINGS**
> Concerning Madonna's wizardry: In point of fact, she rarely uses Still Spell, preferring to strike a pose.

Why shouldn't you kick Otiluke in the junk?

He has resilient spheres.

What's the most magical type of grain?

Spelt.

A new and useful method of organizing spells, included here for the convenience of game masters everywhere: Spells that, devoid of context, sound like sex acts.

- Grasping Hand
- Black Tentacles
- Grease
- Carpet of Adhesion
- Water Weird Stuff
- Flaccid Arrow
- Tenser's Floating Dick
- Color Spray but It Gets in Your Hair
- Friends with Benefits
- Hold Monster Dong
- Pushing Rope Trick
- Goodberries

They say beauty is in the eye of the Beholder,
but they never tell you which one.

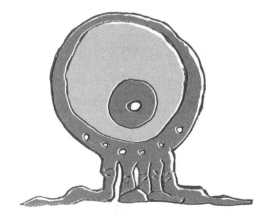

Where is a lich's favorite place to get lunch?

The Cheesecake Phylactery.

> 🔔 **CONCERNING LICHES**
>
> Wouldn't liches actually want to avoid being in the same space as their phylactery?
>
> Theoretically, yes, but have you tried the peanut butter pumpkin? It's so sinful.

What is a dragon's least favorite thing?

A surprise party...of adventurers.

Where would you find a blink dog?

About three feet to the right of where you left them.

 CONCERNING BLINK DOGS
Though members of this breed are friendly and take well to training, beware that this is an energetic breed that will require a great deal of daily teleportation. Additionally, keep an eye out for signs of blink dog hip dysplasia, where the animal's hip teleports without it.

What do you get if you cut the ear off an Owlbear?

An Owlb.

What did the Owlbear say to the rogue?

Nothing. Owlbears don't talk.

What movie had a scene that
got everyone hard?

Basilisk Instinct.

What's worse than finding
a worm in your apple?

Being slowly digested inside the
stomach of a Remorhaz.

How did you hear about the fighter dying?

Remorhaz it.

> 🔔 **CONCERNING THE REMORHAZ**
> I obviously know the right and proper pronunciation of "Remorhaz," which is sort of a giant multilegged worm thing with sword teeth that's found in the snow. In an act of hopefully to-be-remembered magnanimity, I will allow that it might be homologous with "rumor has." (It's not.)

Why didn't the monster ask his crush to prom?

He wasn't Ko-bold enough.

Roll for Initiative:
Roll 2d10 and fill in the blanks.

A _____
[creature]

walks into a bar.

The bartender says,
"Hey, we've got a drink
named after you!"

The _____ says,
[creature]

"Really? You've got a
drink named Murray?"

Dice Roll	Creature
1–12	Zombie
13–20	Vampire
21–29	Obliviax the Memory Moss
30–38	Intellect devourer
39–44	Dire grasshopper
45–55	Thunderbird
56–64	Jersey Devil
65–71	Cerberus
72–78	Ixitxachitl
79–85	1d3 wandering minstrels
86–92	Unicorn
93–100	Yeti

Why couldn't the chimera decide what to eat?

He was of three minds about it.

> ## ⚜ REGARDING THE INTELLIGENCE OF THE CHIMERA
> History's greatest sages have often busied themselves determining if the fearsome chimera, possessing as it does the heads of a goat, lizard, and lion, is in possession of faculties increased by this conglomeration of minds. In fact, no. While two heads may be better than one, three heads seems primarily invested in eating farm animals and getting in fights with itself. Essentially it would not make an ideal bridge partner, unless you hated your opponents.

What sort of people are absolutely necessary for a good game?

Mechanics.

What number really jumps out at you?

3d6.

> 🔔 **ON JOKE CONSTRUCTION**
> Wouldn't this work equally well for any dice arrangement of three? For example, a 3d20 would suffice.
> No one rolls 3d20 for anything; you're overthinking this.
> Someone had to do some thinking here. Any thinking, really.

Where can you find a rules lawyer?

By the book.

Where do 10-sided dice come from?

The Percent Isles.

Our GM refers to his ex as Tunnels and Trolls because she was a real heartbreaker.

🎩 A TREATISE ON THE HEARTBREAKER

Throughout the long history of role-playing games featuring the Something & Something Else naming convention, it has been somewhat chic to try to parrot the largest game in the genre through the release of games that are just like it, except, according to the author, they fix the One Big Problem. This problem can be any number of things, but is generally one of the following: Not religious enough. Not enough fiddly rules. Dwarves do not have an even sillier name. These invariably failed games bear the insider nickname of "heartbreaker." And there you have it. Insider RPG humor, explained.

Why did the min-maxer run to the bathroom?

She had to dump stat.

What do you call it when you take some chips as they pass in front of you?

A snack of opportunity.

Why did the orangutan have trouble getting in character?

Everything he said was OOC.

🎩 **ON THE TOPIC OF ORANGUTAN VOCALIZATIONS**
Once again, I find myself compelled to step in and explain the confusing language this rank amateur employs in the service of humor. *OOC* stands for "out of character," the state in a tabletop game in which players carry on conversations that their characters do not.

Two satyrs are walking along a forest path when they come across a nymph. They hail her, but she's consumed with madness, angrily devouring a handful of dirt and snails while running madly from tree to tree.

"Awesome!" says the first satyr.

"What are you talking about?" asks the second. "This poor creature is suffering!"

"Sure," says the first, "but I do love to find a nymph a maniac."

What noise do overpowered options make?

Splat.

What does a DM's baby learn
to do before it can walk?

Dungeon crawl.

Why was the druid arrested
for trying to summon crows?

Attempted murder.

Roll for Initiative:
Roll 1d100 for Random Cheese Monster Encounter.

Die Roll	Cheesiest Fights
1–12	Air elementaller
13–20	Mummoulette
21–29	Provologre
30–38	Brieholder
39–44	Gorgonzola
45–55	Grue-yere
56–64	Limborcer
65–71	Ixitacheesle
72–78	1d3 wandering Muenstrels
79–85	Kerrygold dragon
86–92	Cheddaaracokra
93–100	Add chips, melt, and roll again

What time do you usually see rogues?

Too late.

🗡 ROGUE APPEARANCE
Is that so, jokester? Because if I never saw another rogue, it would be too soon!

What does a lazy druid do?

The bear minimum.

> ### 🧙 CONCERNING DRUIDS AND WILD SHAPES
> One of the simple truths regarding wielders of ancient druidism is an increased reliance on animal shapes as they progress in power. Part of this is for the power offered by such forms, but convenience must also be taken into consideration. This afore-mentioned lazy druid is likely only even accomplishing this bear minimum so as to poop in the woods.

Did you hear about the halfling who got kicked out of the nudist colony?

He kept poking his nose in everyone's business.

How do gnomes decide what to name their inventions?

Gnomenclature.

Why can't you hear the gnome rogue?

Because that g is silent.

While leaving a tavern, a dwarf
and an elf bump into each other.

"Hey," exclaims the dwarf, "I ain't happy."

"Oh?" replies the elf.
"Then which dwarf are you?"

Why are Svirfneblin such
excellent philosophers?

They're deep gnomes.

🎩 PHILOSOPHY AND GNOMES

As it would happen, Svirfneblin are excellent philosophers, but
not for reasons of jocular wordplay. No, they merely live a very
long time and dedicate a lot of it to looking inward. Because it is
dark where they are and the view is otherwise bad.

A wizard accidentally cursed himself with invisibility. Worried, he ran to the healers to get it removed. Unfortunately, they couldn't see him that day.

How does a gnome create
a pen name for his novel?

He uses a gnome de plume.

Why do gnome-built robots always go crazy?

It's the short circuits.

What happens when you step on a d4?

You take d4 damage.

> 🔔 **DAMAGE FROM IMPROVISED FLOOR WEAPONS—**
> **A THOUGHT**
> The damage done by a d4 on the floor pales in comparison to the
> two toy submarines my son scatters artlessly around the floor.
> They deal subdual damage. Hah! I should have written this book.

Why does everyone like hit points?

They're the life of the party.

Roll for Initiative:
Roll 1d6 for Random Real Life Encounter.

Die Roll	Encounter
1	Slow guy in the fast lane
2	Jane from accounting
3	A friendly dog
4	1d3 wandering minstrels
5	A shop that sells oddly specific items yet seems somehow to stay in business
6	An uncomfortable social media post from your aunt/uncle

What's the biggest problem with a Cloak of Invisibility?

Finding the darn thing.

Why did the man buy an enchanted mattress?

He wanted to bring some magic
back into the bedroom.

 CONCERNING MAGIC MATTRESSES
There are indeed a great number of mattresses of power and
legend. Sadly, the enchantments are often wasted, due to the
magical scourge of incontinent house pets.

What's the best spell to comfort your friend with?

Hold Person.

What do they call ice cream
at the magic academy?

A Cone of Cold.

What's the worst magic item
to take to a solemn event?

A Mace of Disruption.

🎩 **CONCERNING PARTY FOUL BUSINESS**
While technically accurate to the letter of the texts, this ignores
the sheer indignity visited on funerals and will readings by
Murlynd's Novelty Spinning Bow Tie.

What kind of magic item always has weed?

A bag of holdin'.

What magic material is only
heard of in legends?

Myth-ral.

What first-level spell has
the longest duration?

Friends. It lasts about ten seasons.

🎩 SPELL DURATIONS, A TRANSPARENT ACCOUNTING
This is patently ridiculous. First of all, *Friends* lasts your level in
minutes. Second, *Grease* has been touring on and off for nearly
fifty years.

What magic item enhances both your running and chair-throwing abilities?

The Boots of Striding and Springer.

What magic item has the most Bens Grimm in it?

The Deck of Many Things.

> 🎩 **OH, A MARVEL JOKE**
> How inappropriate to the subject matter at hand. Perhaps if this was a reference to *Rat Queens* or *Lumberjanes* it could slide by, but this is just a blatant backdoor pilot for a second book. Crass.

An orc walks into a tavern and begins a bar-room brawl. He knocks several patrons around and generally makes a mess of the place until he sees one patron still just sitting at the bar drinking his beer. "Who are you?" bellows the orc. The man doesn't look up from his drink, and the bartender responds, "Oh, that's just Rodney. He's always here." The orc roars and waves his axe around trying to intimidate Rodney, but he still just sits there drinking. Finally, enraged, the orc charges at the man and bounces right off. "You'd be best just giving up," says the bartender. "That's an Immovable Rod."

Why did the fighter/mage keep asking
everyone to fight her one-on-one?

She was duel classed.

What drink is the most likely
to keep you from harm?

Invisibili-tea.

Why was the game master in such good shape?

He was always the one running.

> **🐌 AN IMPORTANT OBJECTION**
> The above bit of tomfoolery was clearly written by a charlatan!
> No one who has ever met a GM would claim they are in good
> shape. Like many GMs I have known, this cannot stand!

Why are hyperactive monsters so dangerous in early editions of Dungeons & Dragons?

They have 80 HD.

How do you get to

_____?

[location]

Practice!

Die Roll	Location
1	Waterdeep
2	The university of wizards
3	Bard college
4	The nearest dungeon
5	The stocks
6	Avernus
7	A decent prestige class
8	1d3 wandering minstrels
9	The eye of torment, home to one thousand devils and their dark mistress
10	Write a book full of terrible jokes

What RPG does Karl Marx play?

It's just D&D, but he's disabled the class system.

What's worse than raining cats and dogs?

Hailing adventurers!

> 🧙 **SIGNIFICANTLY WORSE! I CONCUR!**
> At least there are people who are happy to have some dogs and cats about.

Why do you never see a
party of vegan adventurers?

They never meat in a tavern.

Why shouldn't you take a
broken spear into a fight?

Well, it's pointless.

What did Sherlock Holmes think of the inner planes?

He found them elementally.

> ⚗ **THE ELEMENTAL PLANES**
>
> You know, don't you, that they've been calling them the Elemental Chaos for years now. It's where slaadi and the like live. Saying "Elemental Planes" is just showing your age.
>
> Then again, it's not like a Sherlock Holmes joke is going to attract anyone under forty either. I suppose you should just carry on as you were.

Where do town guards buy their public humiliation supplies?

The stock market.

Where did the Dark Lord
keep his evil armies?

In his evil sleevies.

The GM told his players there was a
portable hole somewhere in town,
and now they're looking into it.

🧙 **ON THE PORTABLE HOLE**

They very well might be! The core difference between a portable
hole and any other hole adventurers may come across is just the
portability. This is why savvy adventurers will simply try to lift
every hole they encounter off the ground. Better safe than sorry.

Why did the player have her character punch every large rock she came across?

She was trying to hit a milestone.

Why don't cyclopes agree on anything?

They never see eye-to-eye.

Roll for Initiative:
Roll 1d10 for each category to Generate a Character Concept.

Die Roll	Name	Descriptor	Race	Class
1	Brandick	Valiant	Human	Fighter
2	Turtle	Cowardly	Elf	Wizard
3	Gruum'lush	Unfortunate	Half-elf	Monk
4	Tickleberry	Turtle	Half-human	Druid
5	Bill	Meticulous	Halfling	Wrangler
6	Dungus	Curmudgeonly	Half-halfling	Dirt farmer
7	Fauntleroy	Impetuous	Wholeling	Punch witch
8	Sugar Loaf	Doughy	Half-orc	Balloonman
9	Snap Tooth	Pious	Half-and-Half	Accountant
10	Chortlesby	Unbelievably stupid	Turtle	Decker

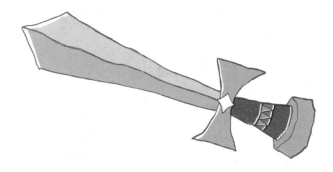

Why did the adventurer want a vorpal sword so badly?

He wanted to get a head in the world.

> 🧙 **CONCERNING THE FAMOUS MUTILATING SWORDS OF OLD**
> He'll need the significantly less famous Sword of Slicing should he wish to instead get a leg up on life.

A wizard shoots a lightning bolt from his magical staff at an enemy. The cleric, wanting to know if he might also use it, asks, "That arcane?"

"No," says the wizard, "that are staff."

The party wizard keeps claiming he's ethereal and can walk through walls, but I think he's just going through a phase.

What kind of dragon enforces the law?

Copper.

> 🧙 **CONCERNING DRAGONS AND THE LAW**
>
> What? No! Copper dragons value freedom and choice above all else. If it's law-loving dragons you're looking for, it's silver that will... Oh, I see. It's a bit of wordplay referencing rickety old vernacular for the police. Honestly, now I'm just curious to see if there's a complementary robber dragon. Probably in one of those "we've gone too far" monster manuals.

When is a turkey a D&D monster?

When it's a'goblin.

What do you call a vampiric goblin?

A hemogoblin.

Why don't dragons like to eat paladins?

They taste lawful.

Why did the ooze stop being emo?

Cutting itself actually did lead to friends.

OOZES, FRIENDS, AND REPRODUCTION
Oozes are something like the worst aspects of the Internet: They can only really stand to be around things exactly as unpleasant as themselves. Thus, their tendency toward mitosis is probably the best-case scenario for everyone, unless they all just sort of stopped forever, I guess.

Why can't you give negative reviews of constructs?

They're immune to criticals.

List of Commonly Used Saves

- Dexterity save
- Constitution save
- Save versus sleep
- Save versus wand, Polymorph, and Grease
- Save Ferris
- Save the whales
- Save your fork; there's pie!

While we were exploring the dungeon, we came across an orc who wouldn't stop asking us questions about life and the universe. I should have known we'd find a wondering monster.

What's the favorite brand of ice cream in the Underdark?

Sahuagin-Dazs.

> **🐌 A GENTLE REBUTTAL**
> Sahuagin-Dazs is certainly of high quality, but in terms of bulk sales numbers, you're going to have a difficult time beating the cheap crap churned out by Driders, and the inexplicable pop-culture success of Ben and Derro's.

Why are Treants not dangerous?

They're all bark and no bite.

Why can't zombies dance?

They just don't have any soul.

Why can't zombies write good music?

They can only de-compose.

> 🎩 **THE SAD TRUTH**
> Also because the Cranberries aren't recording anymore. Oh fiddlesticks, I've saddened myself. Curses!

A dwarf walks into a bar and asks the barkeep for ten shots of strong whiskey, lined up. The bartender, amused, provides the drinks in a neat row. One by one, the dwarf walks down the line and pounds the whiskeys in rapid succession. After the drinks are gone, the bartender says, "That's the most impressive drinking I've ever seen."

"You'd drink like me if you had what I had," responds the taciturn dwarf.

"What've you got?" the barkeep inquires.

"A +3 racial bonus to Constitution saves to resist the effects of poison or strong drink."

What's long and hard and guaranteed
to make you moan?

The Tomb of Horrors.

Where do people buy their giant hammers?

A maul.

How did the peasant react when his flock
was attacked by a dire wolf?

It really got his goat.

Why did the fighter bring his longsword to the wedding?

It was his +1.

Where's the best place to go if you want to fly?

The planes.

> 🎩 **ON THE PLANES**
>
> As opposed to what? Everywhere is the planes, you dolt! You were most likely writing this drivel from the Prime Material. So provincial. Wait, have I become such a pedant? I sound like one of those people who smugly says we're all in space because the planet is in space, or says something about Frankenstein being the doctor and not the monster. These notes are getting away from me.

What does a wizard take when he's sick?

Caster oil.

Why is a cleric like an obedient dog?

It heals on command.

Why didn't the fighter attend the ceremony?

Food poisoning.

Why didn't the rogue attend the ceremony?

Too busy poisoning food.

🗡 **OH GOODY, CONTINUITY**
Oh how droll, one of those series of jokes where the first joke isn't funny until you've also heard the last one. I guess in RPG parlance, jokes prior to this one have been one-shots, and this one counts as a campaign? Like, a campaign of sustained aggression. Against my sensibilities.

What's the difference between a wizard and a sorcerer?

Class.

> **WIZARD OR SORCERER?**
> Strictly speaking, the difference is that one is learned and the other is instinctual. To my mind, both are just weirdos in robes to be avoided if you wish to maintain your bodily integrity.

Why do half-orc bards sound better by candlelight?

There's wax to shove in your ears.

Some adventurers hear a legend of an ancient evil treasure. Hoping to find it, they summon a devil to show them the way. "I don't know where it is, but I know someone who might," says the devil and shows them another summoning ritual. The second devil greets his friend, and the adventurers ask if it knows where the treasure is. The second devil doesn't, but it knows an elder demon who might. When the group summons the elder demon, it says that it knows exactly the place they're talking about and teleports them there in a puff of brimstone. The adventurers open the evil-looking chest in front of them with trepidation only to find it empty. "You tricked us!" cried the party fighter.

"Actually," said the warlock, "I think the real treasure is the fiends we made along the way."

🔔 SUMMONING OF UNDERWORLD DENIZENS

When summoned, fiends aren't actually created by the spell but rather pulled unwilling and aggrieved from the underworld, so technically the party didn't make any fiends. Not with that attitude, anyway.

Why do wizards wear robes?

They got a lot of stares running around naked.

Why can't you tell jokes about a king?

They aren't subjects.

 ON THE RIGHTS AFFORDED KINGS
It's true; they aren't! In fact, it's by divine right they are treated exclusively as predicates in all manners legal and otherwise.

Roll for Initiative:
Roll 1d8 for each category to Randomly Generate an NPC.

Die Roll	Disposition	Descriptor	Profession
1	Friendly	Dirty	Butcher
2	Suspicious	Soiled	Baker
3	Hostile	Grimy	Candlestick maker
4	Uncomfortably friendly	Grubby	Blacksmith
5	Disinterested	Muddy	Silversmith
6	Wary	Filthy	Goldsmith
7	Trusting	Scat-covered	Will Smith
8	Used-cart-salesman-level friendly	Immaculate	Used-cart salesman

What's nine feet long, has six legs, and flies?

Three dead halflings.

Did you hear about that human who was snatched by the undead?

Don't worry, he's all wight now.

> **🎩 THE FURTHER ADVENTURES OF THAT HUMAN**
> In fact, I hear he was later granted the gift of vampirism, where-upon he immediately assumed a mist form. So yes, he's all wight now...in fact, he's a gas.
>   Oh gods, a Rolling Stones reference. I suppose it's on me to forgive you now regarding that Elemental Chaos bit.

What's the most sedentary lycanthrope?

The were-house.

How can you tell your vorpal blade is cheaply made?

Normally they slice off limbs,
but yours is a rip-off.

How does a wizard get his bearings when he goes somewhere new?

He casts Find Familiar.

> 🔔 **ON THE RITUAL OF FINDING A FAMILIAR**
> Indubitable! This could and perchance has even worked in the past!
> Though I would caution the wizard to be quick about it. If he loi-
> ters about while preparing the Find Familiar spell, he's liable to get
> Toad! Ba hah! Watch out, minstrels! I'm coming for your audiences!

What happened when the sorcerers forgot to plan a company meeting till the last minute?

They decided on an Expeditious Retreat.

> 🎩 **FOR THOSE WHO MAY YET BE SEEKING THE JOKE**
> Expeditious Retreat is a spell used by arcanists and the like to increase their ground speed briefly for the purposes of beating a hasty retreat, or more likely, to increase the deadness of their comrades in some way. It has a name only a Brobdingnagian could love, but that's wizards for you. Could have just called it "Run Faster," but obviously that wouldn't sell scrolls.

Why did the adventurer scream when he was grabbed unexpectedly?

It was a Shocking Grasp.

How come wizards don't teleport more often?

The port doesn't listen.

What was the wizard's response when
someone tried to kill him with an illusion?

"Weird."

> ♟ **CONCERNING WEIRDS**
> My goodness, but the authors of this book were convinced that readers would have an encyclopedic knowledge of all matters fantasy. Who remembers what a weird is? I'm 230 years old and have read every treatise concerning magic in existence, and even I start to glaze over when confronted with details from spells above level six. (It's basically a somewhat more amorphous Freddy Krueger. You're welcome.)

A vampire walks into a bar and drops a sack on the table, clearly and plainly labeled, "Noses 4 Sale." The bartender says, "Is that actually a bag of human noses?"

"Well, I reckon mostly human. There's some halfling in there, I think. Two gold each, or I'll trade you a nose fer two ales from yer bar."

The bartender recoils in horror, but eventually curiosity gets the better of him. "Ale is only a silver! Why would you offer that discount?"

"Oh," the vampire says, "It's just my nature. I've always got a nose fer a two."

What's the hottest toy on the plane of Limbo?

The Slip 'n Slaad.

A Sampling of Just a Few of the Abyss's Infinite Planes of Torture

- Plane of Too Many Spiders
- The Pit of Being a Nine-Year-Old and Having to Wear Dress-Up Clothes
- The Realm of Farty Grandmas Who Want to Hug
- A Really Nice House, but the Floors Are Made of d4s
- The Plane of Jef
- A Bed That's Too Cold to Sleep in, but Putting on a Blanket Makes You Too Warm
- The Land of Spikes That You Can Avoid but Are Really Inconveniently Placed
- The Wailing Valley of High-Pitched Baby Screams
- An Entire Plane of Just This Book As the Only Entertainment

There was a gathering of all the giant races that lasted late into the night. As it went on, one by one the various races began to leave until only one was left. Then they shrugged and decided to go home because it was all ogre.

———

What makes the best Gothic statue polish?

Gargoyle.

Why wasn't the master of metallic dragons afraid of anything?

He had big brass ones.

What do you say if someone asks if you can act like a tiny tinkerer?

"I don't gnome."

What do you say if someone asks if you can act like a hyena-man?

"I don't Gnoll."

How does a sphinx start its bedtime prayers?

"Now I lamia down to sleep..."

> **A PRONUNCIATION GUIDE TO LAMIA**
> For this joke to work, you would need to pronounce it "LAY-me-uh" instead of "Luh-me-uh." This is a bit problematic, given the original Greek. Also, you would need to accept the idea that a sphinx says prayers at bedtime.

Why did the dragon eat the will-o'-the-wisp?

He wanted a light snack.

Why is it hard to read
a warlock's handwriting?

It's all in cursive.

Did you hear about the rogue who owed
money to chiropractors all over town?

He had a massive backstab.

What do you call a minotaur's big brother?

A maxotaur.

What do you call a juice that causes paralysis?

Ghoul-Aid.

What kind of scam does a flying monster run?

A hippo-grift.

> ⚓ **ON FLYING LARCENY**
> The hippo-grift is really just an outsized form of the dire pigeon
> drop, which is itself just a two-man variation of three-card Mon-
> tecore. Yes, it's a rich and varied tradition of pun crimes.

How does a water elemental say hello?

It waves.

⚑ REGARDING ELEMENTAL GREETINGS

There may be some curiosity about the greeting forms of the other elemental varieties. Well, you're lucky I'm here, as this is the sort of useless horse-quackery I specialize in knowing. Earth elementals go for the handquake, air elementals just sort of breeze past you, and fire elementals burn down your house.

How many adventurers does it take to change a light bulb?

All of them! Don't split the party.

How many clerics
does it take to change a light bulb?

Just one. They can Cure Light.

How many paladins
does it take to change a light bulb?

One to get the replacement;
one to uphold the light.

> **⚱ LIGHT BULB JOKES**
> So it's come to this. Very well, I shall retire for the evening to administer my night tinctures and study the great, and actual, humorists of history.

Roll for Initiative:
Roll 1d8 and fill in the blanks for a Tragic Backstory.

My ＿＿＿＿＿＿＿＿＿＿ was
[first blank]

＿＿＿＿＿＿＿＿＿＿
[second blank]

by ＿＿＿＿＿＿＿＿.
[third blank]

Die Roll	First Blank	Second Blank	Third Blank
1	Mother	Stolen	Goblins
2	Father	Killed	Rampaging peasants
3	House	Slightly inconvenienced	1d3 wandering minstrels
4	Sibling	Abandoned	Three gnomes in a trench coat
5	Favorite pet	Sold into slavery	Intense guilt
6	Priceless heirloom	Disappointed	Me
7	Self	Dunked on	Elminster
8	Child	Clowned	Gummy Jim the Toothless

We have a chaotic evil paladin
whom we nicknamed Life Alert
because he's fallen and he can't get up.

> **🎩 REGARDING THE ANTI-PALADIN**
> Very well then, I have executed a proper wake up and breakfast. I
> hope we are through with the frivolities of light bulb jokes. Now,
> to the task at hand. This joke is older than my great-uncle's teeth,
> and he is the first and eldest dragon of order. Shall I put a kettle
> on while you ready your joke regarding the location of the beef?

A man walks into a bard. The bard says,
"What is this, some kind of joke?"

Why is it hard to have a conversation around a Tiefling?

They're always horning in.

> **🗿 CONSIDERING THE TIEFLING**
> Personally, I've always found Tieflings trying while at cocktail gatherings and sacred rituals, because no matter how interesting your story, they always seem to have a tail to top it.

Why couldn't the druid get around town?

He was stuck in neutral.

I had trouble believing the party rogue was stealing tavern placards, but when I checked his house, the signs were all there.

It's hard to explain metaphors to rogues because they're always taking things, literally.

How can you tell your party bard has slept with every guy in this tavern?

His display of bar dick knowledge.

> 🧙 **REGARDING THE ANTICS OF THE PARTY BARD**
> Ah, the eternal dance of flesh and sinew. The filthy parade of skin on skin that your party bard invariably turns each otherwise casual and potentially enthralling evening at your local drinking establishment into. Frankly, I find his lust all just so much frippery. Relax, my old friend, there will always be "dudes on the dance floor."

The enemy wizard didn't
want me to cast Feeblemind on him,
but I managed to change his mind.

What happened when the cleric forgot to
prepare Light?

It was a dark time.

I thought the enemy only had level-two spells, but then he cast Lightning Bolt at me. I was really shocked.

A TREATISE ON LEVELS AND THEIR APPLICATION

It is a well-worn truism that casters and those who need to work alongside them need to track multiple meanings of the term "level." A fifth-level wizard has at his disposal third-level spells. This confusing issue could have been clearly cleaned up with the addition of even a single synonym and has historically been laid at the feet of spendthrift creation-era accountancy. I would have suggested that characters have levels and spells have ranks, but what do I know? Oh yes, everything.

Did you hear about the wizard who accidentally cast Silence on his wife?

She isn't talking to him.

What do you tell a wizard who constantly tries to magically unlock every door she comes to?

Don't Knock it till you try it.

THE KNOCK SPELL, ELUCIDATED

Knock, of course, opens any door that is closed and barred by nonmagical means. Casting it on unlocked doors accomplishes nothing save wasting your precious spell slots, and casting it on locked doors makes your party's rogue feel a right tit. Worth it to some, I imagine.

A transmuter battling foes accidentally transmogrifies everyone but himself into cheap wooden chairs. Unable to reverse the spell and distraught, he drags his furniture friends home to his city and begs the local church to render aid. The head cleric says, "Well, our plan of action is to put pillows on them."

"Will that cure them?" the transmuter inquires.

"Oh no," says the cleric. "At this stage, all we can do is make them comfortable."

🧙 ON THE USAGE OF POLYMORPH

Polymorph has a natural duration, you know. In a few hours, those chairs will become adventurers again, covered in layers of pillows and confused friars. It'll be downright horrifying if any of the adventurers were raised in religious institutions.

Why did the wizard's Staff of Power
start to hum?

It didn't know the words.

What did the dragon say after being hit by a vorpal sword?

Thanks for halving me!

List of Available Rogue Subclasses

- Scoundrel
- Ruffian
- Ne'er-do-well
- Thief
- No-goodnick
- Skullduggerist
- Middle manager
- Jef
- Jerkwad
- Total jackwagon
- Boatman on the River Dicks

What's green and sounds like a dork?

An orc.

How does a snake-man offer you tea?

"Yuan-ti?"

🐍 **ON THE HABITS OF THE YUAN-TI**

These devious snake people are first and foremost unlikely to offer you tea. As a matter of fact, they'd likely prefer to bisect you with a bloody great scimitar and offer your charred remains to some god resembling a pile of snakes. Even if tea is proffered, it is likely poisoned (with the oh so jejune and predictable snake venom). It's best to refuse it, and honestly, who wouldn't? How does poisoned tea made out of boiled mouse sound, flavor-wise?

What kind of monster develops one strength to the exclusion of all else?

A min-maxotaur.

What's the best way to find out who the most popular centaur is?

A Gallop poll.

Why don't mimics make very good chairs?

No opposable thumbs, for one.

What's the most festive undead creature?

A Christmas wraith.

REGARDING SIMILAR FESTIVITIES AND THE ANIMATED DECEASED
Once again, I must protest as to the uneducated nature of the author. Has he no awareness whatsoever of those who practice other faiths? What about the mummynorah?

How did they balance
the Beholder this edition?

They just eyeballed it.

Did you know Beholders are polyamorous?

They're always seeing multiple people.

Roll for Initiative:
Roll 1d100 for Treasure.

Die Roll	Treasure Received
1–10	A magical top
11–16	Two bards with long beards
17–20	One bard with no beard
21–35	Scroll of Tush Location
36–50	Assorted jewelry (gold watch, diamond ring, etc.) worth 2d1,000 gp
51–60	Legs (Use Magic Device check required to know how to use them)
61–75	Musical instrument
76–85	The deed to a country house with farm buildings attached
86–95	Cheap sunglasses (10 percent chance of being magical)
96–100	Roll twice and ignore any further rolls of this result

An adventuring party finds a pile of treasure at the end of a dungeon. The wizard sees a staff and gets excited about the prospect of a new magic item. She picks it up and begins trying to use it, but every time she does, a booming voice says, "This treatment is unfair! No work without fair wages!" and nothing happens.

Confused, she takes it back to town to be identified. The sage she takes it to looks at it for a bit and then says, "I see the problem. This is a Staff of Striking."

What do you call the dragon who ate your entire adventuring company?

A real party pooper.

Where does a mage keep her mage clothes?

In her Mage Armoires.

How was the scholar able to get to the dungeon before the rest of the party?

She really booked it.

How do you measure the radius of a horse-man?

First, you have to find the centaur and work out from there.

> **🔔 ON CENTAURS AND MATHEMATICS**
> To measure the height of a centaur is much simpler; you only need your hands! Hah, get it? Because of how horses are measured to the shoulder?
>
> No, that was terrible. I'm beginning to see why you wrote this book, and I am merely taking notes.

Why did the mage's familiar keep sticking to things?

It was a Vel-Crow.

> ### 🎩 ON MAGE'S FAMILIARS
> Quite frankly, these nasty little things are usually pretty sticky-fingered to begin with. I can't tell you the number of times I've had to retreat indoors to protect my summer picnic meals from roving packs of flying tomes and curious toads. One assumes they're only receiving dry food at home, or worse, illusory wet food.

What spell is the corniest?

Maze.

Roll for Initiative:

Roll 1d8 for Alternate Effects for the Casting of Prismatic Spray.

Die Roll	Color	Effect
1	Red	Hearts appear in the target's eyes, and it is charmed
2	Orange	A pot of gold worth 2d100 gp deals 10d6 crushing damage
3	Yellow	Stars swirl and blast the target for 10d6 radiant damage
4	Green	Target is covered in clovers that act as a Bane spell
5	Blue	Moonbeams shine down, dealing 10d6 cold damage
6	Indigo	Target is pinned to the ground by horseshoes and is considered grappled for 1d10 rounds
7	Violet	Balloons attach themselves to the target, and it is affected as per the Reverse Gravity spell
8	Rainbow	Target is struck twice; roll twice more, rerolling any 8s

An adventuring party brings their injured and crazed friend to a cleric for assistance. The cleric examines the man and casts a few spells before declaring, "Well, he's got vampirism, mummy rot, lycanthropy, basilisk poison, and a geas on him. Plus, all his equipment is just cursed like crazy."

The party asks what can possibly be done, and the cleric responds, "Oh, that's easy, we'll put him in a room on a diet of flounder and hardtack."

"Will that cure all those diseases?" the party asks.

"Oh no. They'll just fit under the door."

Why did the party ask
if the diviner was feeling okay?

He was scrying.

I accidentally cast Chill Touch on my friend,
and now they're giving me the cold shoulder.

CHILL TOUCH AND FRIENDSHIP
Chill Touch can indeed put a little frost on a relationship, as it deals painful cold damage to its target. But what's a little real damage between friends? Like, one point of damage?

Why was the necromancer living alone?

His wight left him.

Why don't druids ever get blamed for farts?

They Pass Without Trace.

Why are Beholders considered attractive?

They are so good-looking.

What's a Treant's favorite soda?

Root beer.

ON TREANTS

Though it's largely true that the majority of Treants enjoy root beer when imbibing carbonated sugar treats, there are a few as well who prefer birch beer, a disgusting and real beverage I cannot recommend. Worse still are the few who willingly trade on *eBay* for bottles of that horrible soda that tasted of Christmas tree.

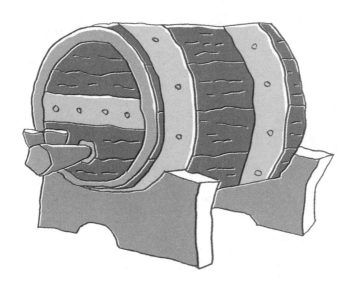

Why did the sorcerer never cast Web?

It always left him in a sticky situation.

Why are role-players so trustworthy?

They have character.

Why did the druid beat up
the trespassing monster?

It was in his nature.

Did you hear about the fighter who broke apart his armor and sent it to ten friends?

It was chain mail.

 SCAMS AND THE FANTASY WORLD

Chain mail scams are one of the most common and unfortunate bits of swindlery that affects the realms of fantasy and adventure. Less common but far more dangerous are those insidious mummies and their pyramid schemes.

Did you hear about the gathering of the barbarians?

It was a real rager.

I wasn't sure if I wanted to prepare Levitate, but it has its ups and downs.

✦

What spell does a witch cast
when she needs to get away?

Witch Bolt.

Our mage found a cursed book,
and she just can't put it down.

> ### 🎩 CONCERNING CURSED TOMES
> You needn't worry; your arcanist will be perfectly fine. The vast majority of accursed writings can be relinquished freely once the unlucky target has completed their reading. Oh...but I see the book is *Infinite Jest*. Have you considered hiring a new mage? Let me give you my card.

Why did the Mind Flayer call off from work?

He was Ill-ithid.

Roll for Initiative:
Roll 1d6 and fill in the blanks to Generate a Setting for Your Campaign.

The _____ of

[first blank]

_____ is

[second blank]

beset by _____.

[third blank]

Die Roll	First Blank	Second Blank	Third Blank
1	Kingdom	Dungsberry	Swearing Kobolds
2	Duchy	Frontbottom	Goblins on corgis
3	Barony	Pantsford upon Avon	1d3 wandering minstrels
4	Principality	Widdle-on-Thames-cum-Snodsberry	Adventurers
5	Commonwealth	Giggleswick upon Humber	Jef
6	People's Republic	St. Melonsby	Malarkey

Why can only the bravest
bards play the harp?

It takes a lot of pluck.

Why did the minstrel start singing
at the horse?

He was told it needed barding.

Why did the rogue always pickpocket bards?

They have the best lute.

🧙 BARDS AND INSTRUMENTS
Bards also have the best glockenspiels, French horns, crwths, sackbuts, and ocarinas. But you try fitting those into a joke. Actually, wait, sackbut seems pretty easy. No one make a sackbut joke; I call dibs.

What does a spellcaster use
to protect her valuables?

A war-lock.

An elf, a human, and a halfling decide to go to
a tavern to relax. When the bill comes, they
each dig through their pockets to find the
money they need. The halfling is a little short.

What does a fighter say when he's in a bad mood?

"Cleave me alone."

> **⚔ THE PARADOX OF THE INTROVERTED FIGHTER**
>
> The poor warrior in this anecdote... You are aware, of course, that *cleave* literally describes the process of hitting one target and then continuing through with the swing to hit another target as well. This unfortunate fellow is seeking solitude but must find at least two people he wants nothing to do with in order to achieve it!

What do you get if you boil a bard?

A skald.

What does a monk use to clock in for work?

A punch card.

I used to date an older Warforged
but had to dump him because
he was too high maintenance.

The rogue managed to steal from the butcher's shop without getting caught by using a little sleight of ham.

New Wondrous Magical Items

- Boots of Slipping and Sliding
- The Deck of One or Two Things
- Stationary Hole
- Movable Rod
- Girdle of Giant Feet
- Kimono of Appropriation
- Insufferable Fedora
- Goggles of Intoxication
- Cloak of Half-Elven, Kind Of

Why do lords always make the decisions about parties?

Because the ball is in their court.

Why did the RPG manufacturer remove so much from the latest edition?

They just had to get it out of their system.

> **⚖ CONCERNING EDITION CHANGES**
> Traditionally, the reason that a new edition is smaller than the previous edition is that the writers are tasked with stripping the game down to its basics in service of selling you everything interesting again. Though recently, there's an argument that the new edition was stripped down out of fear of the previous edition's potency and might.

An angry-looking dwarf walks into a bar brandishing flint and steel menacingly. The bartender says to him, "Okay, I'll let you in... but don't start anything."

Why was the brazen strumpet who plied
her wares near the jousting arenas so busy?

Well, she worked most knights.

What do you call a rogue
with a lot of hit points?

A CON artist.

Why was it hard for the ranger
to walk anywhere?

He had fallen archers.

Why do barbarians love
dealing damage so much?

It's all the rage.

What does a warlock use
to plan his battles?

A Hex grid.

🎩 WARLOCK MAGIC
Oh, I see we're involving the somewhat more obscure collection
of warlock spells now. This is lovely. Can't wait for a Hunger of
Hadar pun or something about being hurled through hell. Those
guys are always so dramatic about everything.

Roll for Initiative:
Roll 1d10 and fill in the blank to Make Your Own Terrible Joke!

Take my

———————— .

Please!

Die Roll	Blank
1	Knife
2	Hireling
3	Hand, and let's run away together
4	Copper pieces
5	1d3 wandering minstrels
6	Cursed armor
7	Hit points
8	Jef
9	DVD of the 2000 film *Dungeons & Dragons*
10	Advice, and just get out of here

Why do people prefer to live near thieves' guilds?

Good fences make good neighbors.

> **🔔 ON THE TOPIC OF FENCES**
> This joke relies on the double meaning of the term "fence," in this instance referring to a criminal who makes a living by purveying stolen goods. Indeed, in this case, a fence would make an excellent neighbor; say, for example, if your bike is regularly stolen and you appreciate convenience in the matter of buying it back from the accomplice of those who pilfered it from you in the first place.

I once met a woman who polished plate mail at home as a hobby and as a way to meet eligible paladins. She was always looking for a night in, shining armor.

What sport do you play with a werebat?

Were.

What does the rogue choose
for his bagel toppings?

He picks lox.

🔔 **ON FELONIOUS TOPPINGS**
The well-to-do and successful rogue will also not be averse to a
few capers, if you catch my drift.

You know why the Plane of Fire always throws the best parties?

It's lit.

Why do undead wizards never progress beyond demilich?

It's important to quit **when you're ahead.**

🎩 **REGARDING THE DEMILICH**
For the uninitiated, a demilich is a lich (already a powerful undead wizard) who has passed beyond even that degree of might, becoming a creature of little more than skull, jewels, and raw magical power. Sometimes they also marry Ashton Kutcher.

What kind of insects can a cleric turn?

Zombees.

The fighter wanted to improve
his combat readiness so he decided to
attend an Armor class.

What's a kraken's favorite food?

Fish and ships.

An adventuring party manages to sneak up on a werewolf guarding a treasure, but they find the beast engaged in licking his own nuts. The fighter nudges the party wizard and says, "I wish I could do that."

The wizard responds, "Go ahead; he looks pretty friendly."

Why do dragons have tiny balls?

They're pretty bad dancers.

> 🔔 **DRAGONS AND DANCING**
> You may have previously heard that in fact some dragons are phenomenal dancers. There is an old saying that addresses this. If the dragon can dance, and it was on *Degrassi*, then that's no dragon, friend. You're looking at a Drake.

Why don't Formians get sick?

They have anty bodies.

> **🐌 THE FORMIAN**
> To the true beginner, this joke may appear simply as a bit of nonsense. Only the true Dungeoneers will recall that the Formian is a sort of ant-person occasionally found in deadly dungeons or caves. They have ant bodies. Please don't confuse them with fomorians, which are a type of hideous fey giant. Which would ruin the joke.

Why did the barbarian add a story to his house?

He wanted to gain a level.

The

_____ & _____ .

[first blank]   [second blank]

Die Roll	First Blank	Second Blank
1	Toad	Jerkin
2	Peasant Footman	Slop
3	Knob	Sewer Rat
4	Bucket	King's Casual
5	Queen's Fancy	Jef
6	Otyugh	Son of a Bitch
7	Cock	Catastrophe
8	Drunk	Chunk

What's the best way to kill a Treant?

Whittle by whittle.

🔔 **A MORDANT TREATISE ON TREANT MURDER**
Honestly, virtually any form of murder or violence that would ter-minate a human or tree will work acceptably well in the situation of the Treant. As tough and wooden as they appear to be, it is a rough lot to be susceptible to both the common cold and Dutch elm disease.

What's a Treant's favorite TLC song?

"No Shrubs."

What sport are rangers best at?

Track.

🎩 **RANGERS AND SPORTS**
All jests aside, wouldn't rangers be better at archery? They seem
pretty bow-y in my admittedly limited experience.

It turns out most small businesses are started by rogues. They have the most initiative.

What do you call a retired wizard?

A was-ard.

The fighter walked up to the barbarian after the fight and said, "Hey, that axe of yours is pretty impressive!"

"Thanks," said the barbarian, "it's a greataxe."

> 🎩 **BARBARIAN WEAPONRY**
> Did you know this joke would also work with a greatsword? It would! Feel free to substitute when sharing the joke among your friends or neighbors. Or just tell this joke twice in a row with the substituted weapon. Results are guaranteed!

What do high-level monks eat before a race?

Nothing. They fast.

How do halfling barbers work so fast?

They use a lot of shortcuts.

> 🎩 **HALFLINGS AND THE BARBER**
> In truth, the speed of halfling barbers is born of necessity. Any work they do on the head must be repeated twice more on each of the little blighters' hairy feet. Have you ever seen a halfling walking around on a fresh new set of pageboys? It is disturbingly adorable.

What kind of elves get the worst grades?

Aquatic elves. They're always below sea level.

What sound did the piano
that fell on a dwarf make?

A-flat minor.

How did the psionicist always know what
people got him for his birthday?

He felt their presents.

🎩 THE ONLY PSIONICIST JOKE
We had to have one. Turns out there's always one weird player
who wants these guys involved in the game for some reason.

XP Earned for Heroic Actions

XP Earned	Action Taken
25	Use a skill successfully
50	Role-play with an NPC instead of killing them
100	Role-play with another player instead of killing them
200	Make a sacrifice for the greater good
250	Make a sacrifice for the greatest good
500	Remember any ridiculous fantasy names without checking notes
1,000	Successfully not derail the adventure
10,000	Give the DM a pizza

What kind of monster is always losing stuff?

A Misplacer Beast.

What's the most effective
contraception among orcs?

Seeing in the dark.

Why are Gnolls so bad at stealth?

They are always spotted.

The bard kept playing a song to make sure the fighter didn't forget about the time he broke her stringed instrument. She just kept harping on about it.

What do storm giants wear
under their clothes?

Thunderwear.

What part of a dragon weighs the most?

The scales.

What did the dragon say when it was grabbed by the tip of its tail?

"Well, that's the end of me."

> 🔔 **DRAGONS AND SARCASM**
> Naturally, this is just what the dragon says before whipping around and eating you. It's...not like they have a glowing weak spot back there. Unless they're the rare Atari dragon. If it is, then go nuts, I suppose.

If an iron golem and a gold golem team up, what do you call them?

Alloys.

Why won't Blibdoolpoolp share?

She's pretty shellfish.

 A MUCH-NEEDED EXPLANATION ABOUT THE GOD OF KUO-TOA
To understand this joke, you'll either need to acquire and peruse a copy of an old copy of *Deities & Demigods* or simply trust me. She is a giant naked lady with pincers and a crawdad for a head. It's unsettling, to say the very least.

How can you tell there's a winged legendary cat-man in a dark room?

Because it sphinx in there.

Did you hear about the druid who survived an adventure alone just using a magic lamp and Conjure Woodland Beings spells?

He had to djinn and bear it.

Did you hear about the two bloodsuckers who fought till they both died?

It was a vam-pyrrhic victory.

The paladin is looking into the theft of his horse, but so far, he has nothing to go on.

Where do seahorses go to school?

On a hippocampus.

🎩 **HIPPOCAMPUS DISAMBIGUATION**
To those well versed in anatomy, we are talking about the fish/ horse monster. I don't think the author would want to imply that mythical seahorses have schools on giant brains.

Roll for Initiative:
Roll 1d6 for each column to Randomly Generate a New Orc Tribe for Your Setting.

Die Roll			
1	Narsty	Foot	Clan
2	Bloody	Tooth	Tribe
3	Grubby	Nose	Society
4	Bitey	Grubbins	Friends
5	Scabby	Baby	Hooligans
6	Reasonable	Flower	Commune

Why is a broken drum the best instrument for a bard?

It can't be beat.

Why don't halflings get jokes?

The punch lines go over their heads.

> 🎩 **IN DEFENSE OF THE HALFLING**
> You know what, I'm getting a little perturbed at all these jokes at the expense of the halflings and their height. In fact, I've had it up to here with them!
> You couldn't see it, but my hand was like three feet off the ground.

I saw a big gathering of halflings the other day with a lone hobbit in the middle of it. He seemed to be the Tolkien minority.

Did you hear about the wizard whose cheap Polymorph scrolls only turned people into halflings?

He was shortchanged.

Why shouldn't you hire a halfling to be your chef?

The steaks are just too high!

HALFLINGS AGAIN?
I simply must insist that this is the end of these interminable jokes on the diminutive stature of halflings! You know, they bear many other sterling, admirable qualities! They can...whistle better than most...and they have good aim...with rocks. Still, this must indeed be the terminus of these japes.

Why are halflings good folks?

They don't look down on people.

> 🔔 **OH, FOR THE LOVE OF YONDALLA!**
> Fine. Do as you will. I'm going to the tavern for the evening.

Why don't halflings ever get mugged?

No criminal would stoop so low.

What has two butts and kills people?

An ass ass in.

How does a ranger tie his shoes?

With a longbow.

> **🔔 RANGERS AND FOOTWEAR**
> Rangers are traditionally a hearty lot who tend to craft their own clothes, and footwear is no exception. You can always tell a ranger in a crowd. He'll be dressed as a hunter with a bow, and he'll be wearing boots with fur.

What do you say to a fey beast
you're in a staring contest with?

"Blink, dog."

How did the rogue stop other thieves from
getting into his territory?

He bandit.

🧎 ROGUES, BANDITS, AND HIGHWAYMEN
A single rogue probably lacks the wherewithal to completely ban other thief activity from his territory. Indeed, kings can't seem to accomplish that, and they're nominally in charge of everyone.

What did the paladin's mom say when he finally settled down for bed?

"Good knight."

New Profession Skills for Players

- Grave borrower
- Bug eater
- Outhouse technician
- Baby scolder
- Dungeon viscera cleaner
- Elephant puncher
- Orc snot collector
- Insurance adjuster

My new favorite underground band plays the best music. It's Lizardfolk.

Our party was worried
that there were mimics around,
but the table assured us
it was perfectly safe.

🎩 **MIMICS!**

Mimics are disgusting little creatures that can assume the shape of virtually anything. They wait quietly to ambush unsuspecting adventurers. Of course, an adventurer has to be unusually unsuspecting, what with the mimics' teeth and massive slavering tongues. Mimics are largely responsible for the unpopularity of Gothic- or Halloween-themed furniture design the world over!

What's an Englishman's favorite monster?

Black Pudding.

> 🔔 **THE BRITISH AND THE MONSTER**
> There's in fact a long and fine tradition of British monsters being named for food, from the stalwart toad in the hole to the dire spotted dick, a monster that should be avoided at all costs.

Did you hear about the multiheaded monster who loved to grow plants?

It was super into hydra-ponics.

What's the difference between
a rakshasa and a house cat?

One is a conniving feline monster
and the other has backward hands.

What's the most refreshing fey creature?

A sprite.

What kind of crackers do elementals like?

Firecrackers.

What did the werewolf say when the heroes barged in on him?

"Don't look! I'm changing."

> 🐌 **CONCERNING WEREWOLVES**
> Werewolves often find themselves in the throes of sartorial distress. Their lycanthropic transformations do tend to tear and rend garments away from them, paradoxically leaving them with nothing to wear. Wear-wolf. Ha ha! Again, I am become the joke smith!

How do you stop a minotaur from charging?

Cancel his credit cards.

Why should you swipe left on the undead?

The chance of getting ghosted is too high.

> 👻 **UNDEAD AND DATING APPS**
> However, one must bear in mind that ghosts, being incorporeal, take no meaningful damage from being swiped in any direction, unless your dating app is +1 or forged on a cell phone of cold iron.

Why shouldn't you bother a Treant before noon?

Morning wood is just so embarrassing.

Roll for Initiative:
Roll 1d10 for each column to Generate a Creature for Summoning Spells.

Die Roll	Descriptor	Type
1	Fiendish	Badger
2	Dire	Wolverine
3	Celestial	Ooze
4	Ghost	Duck
5	Vampiric	Fiend
6	Gelationous	Vampire
7	Awkward	Wombat
8	Useless	Cube
9	Roll twice more and keep both; reroll 9 or 10	Jef
10	Roll three more times and keep both; reroll 9 or 10	Ghost

Why didn't the frog paladin fall off the ledge?

Good grippli.

Did you hear about the illusionist who married an invisible stalker?

Their kids were nothing to look at.

> ### 🗿 INVISIBLE STALKERS
> Invisible stalkers simply never have any visible form; they are born (created, really) invisible and remain that way throughout their lives. If there is a married one out there in the world, it must have a spectacular personality.

Why is a ninth-level spellcaster the best dominatrix?

She can Dominate Person several times per day.

A group of monsters were chasing after a couple gnomes. Thinking quickly, one told the other to hide in his unfinished flying machine. The monsters passed them by without seeming to see them at all.

"That was amazing," said the other gnome. "How did you know it would work?"

"Well," said the first gnome, "monsters can't find you in a demiplane."

What warning did the necromancer give his partner before getting intimate?

Eyebite.

Why was the assassin in bed all day?

He was working undercover.

🎩 ASSASSINS ON THE JOB
Assassins have been known to remain perfectly still for hours or even days at a time to accomplish a hit on a valuable target. Indeed, it can be said that the only real difference between the employed and unemployed assassin is a few minutes at the end of the day.

Why did the gnomes lose their mining contract?

Just totally dwarfed by the competition.

> 🧙 **DWARVES AND MINING NEGOTIATION**
> This is distressingly common. Dwarves maintain an ironclad motto that poor gnomes seeking to break into the industry have difficulty working around: "If it's dwarves, it's mine."

Why wouldn't the child talk to the archer?

She had been warned of ranger danger.

Why can't wizards get kisses at Christmas?

The Magic Missile-Toe moves too fast.

Did you hear about the warlock who tried to defend his infernal pact?

He was just playing Devil's Advocate.

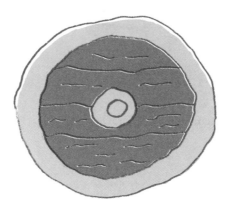

The paladin had a steed that was too big for him to dismount while in full armor. He just couldn't seem to get off his high horse.

🔔 **PALADINS AND WARHORSES**

Did you know that paladins who summon their faithful and holy mounts occasionally may not receive the horse they expected? I once knew a fellow whose holy charge stuck him with a giraffe—which meant he also had to haul around a ladder. Lost a fortune trying to bard that thing too.

Why was the bard angry at the rogue who entered his talent contest?

He really stole the show.

Adventuring Supplies That No Player Should Be Without

- Barrel of pickled herring
- Sealant wax and ring
- Big ol' bag of sand
- Trunk of tax returns
- Full dinette set with fondue pot
- Three different journals you'll definitely get around to writing in
- Soap on a fifty-foot length of silk rope
- 1d3 wandering Jefs
- Poles of varying length
- Caravan to hold all this crap

How do you know an
air elemental liked your joke?

They thunderclap.

Why do you get so sweaty when a ton of rats are around?

It's swarm.

🔥 SWARMS OF THINGS

In a game, you can call things in a swarm whenever it would be useful to categorize creatures that are attacking en masse. While it is generally applied to diminutive (and prone to swarming) creatures, such as rats, bats, and the like, there's nothing in most rulebooks that says a party can't face down a swarm of elephants. Once the battle is done, characters'll be welcome to search for treasure among a great heaving pile of fallen elephants and elephant leavings. Glorious indeed.

Why don't vampires like to feed on royalty?

There's always a long bloodline.

What do you call a shocked undead?

A ghast.

What is the most popular
delivery app for the undead?

Ghostmates.

Where do all the shapeshifters
hang out at the mall?

The changeling rooms.

What do you call a dire wolf with
particularly short legs?

A worgi.

🎩 **THE ADORABLY DIRE**
Beware should you seek one of these chubby ambulatory doom
footballs as your steed or pet. Though fiercely loyal, they are
prone to dire hip dysplasia, and their battle cry, while loud indeed,
is more bork than bark.

What do you call a gorgeous orc bodyguard
who has trouble making friends?

A pretty awkward pretty orc ward.

What's the only monster
you can bring on an airline?

A carrion crawler.

🪄 RULES AND STIPULATIONS

If you do choose a carrion crawler for your aerial accompaniment, watch out that he hasn't recently fed. Or, if feeding is simply unavoidable, that you squeeze him clean of all but about three ounces of blood or other bodily juices.

What kind of car does a GM drive?

Fiat.

What mountain do players scale to gain a level?

Experience Point.

> ♟ **A HILARIOUS REJOINDER**
> Oh! I've got one! I wish to participate, however briefly, in this chicanery! The answer to your question is actually Mountain Dew! Hah! You remember, from the Internet and gaming culture in general?

How can you tell a

_____ is lying?
[creature]

You can see right through them!

Die Roll	Creature
1	Ghost
2	Invisible stalker
3	Vampire currently in mist form
4	Wizard's astral projection
5	Gelatinous cube
6	Glass golem
7	Egg held up to the light
8	Goblin who has managed to get translucent somehow

What do you call a yeti who's especially insulting?

A sassquatch.

🎩 OF MATTERS SASSQUATCH

Having spent a small amount of time among these snappy and inventive folk, I can also inform readers of discernment that they universally follow a singular matriarchal leader, the Yassquatch Queen.

What do you call a yeti with a six-pack?

An abdominable snowman.

What happened when the fighter got disarmed?

Things really got out of hand.

What happens to wizards who get caught drunk driving?

Their license is evoked.

🧙 OTHER OPTIONS PROVIDED

No, no, no! They're hauled before an abjury of their peers! Or... they are summoned to traffic school! Hang on, I'm sure there's one for illusion. I'll get there.

Why didn't the sorcerer stick around after Fireballing the merfolk?

He had bigger fish to fry.

Did you know that low-level bards are often paid in strips of dragonhide?

It's true—until they make a name for themselves, they're generally stuck working for scale.

Did you hear about the Kenku at the underground dance party?

He was raven the entire time.

> **🔔 THE KENKU**
> This was somewhat more common in the nineties. Oh, how the Kenku would flock to converted warehouses, resplendent in their stripey top hats and thick layers of candy necklaces. Nowadays, it's all perfectly mimicking the voices of their enemies and munching avocado toast.

What slime multiplies
into a gelatinous cube?

A gelatinous cube root.

What do you call a gelatinous cube
with a drinking problem?

A gelatinous cuba libre.

An adventuring party is wandering through a large art museum. As they pass a painting depicting a classical battle, the bard points it out and announces it as "a fine example of neoclassical tableau." While looking about the elven art exhibits, he spots and proclaims a fine crystalline sculpture, "a work of neomodern aquatic elf statuary." Then, while walking through the displays of orcish works, he points to a large lump of garbage, but before he can identify it, it promptly sprouts tentacles, grabs him, and devours him on the spot. "What the hell was that?" cries the terrified wizard, and the fighter replies, "Fine example of a neo-Otyugh."

🏛 THE NEO-OTYUGH AS ART STATEMENT

Something like 80 percent of readers won't know that an Otyugh is a lumpen flesh mass that lives in garbage to ambush the unsuspecting with its foul tentacles, and of them, even a smaller portion will know that you call a bigger one a "neo-Otyugh," for some reason! Besides that, how many people are familiar with neoclassical tablature? Won't anyone consider the reader?

Why do giant birds hate journalism?

Because papers beat rocs.

A horned fellow just threw his cup of Earl Grey at me! You know what, I should have expected it from a Tiefling.

🎩 **THE TIEFLING**
These brimstone-scented bad boys and girls are always flinging something. Usually hellfire, often daggers, and yes, sometimes, tea. The name, however, is a coincidence. What is the word "Tiefling" really about? Well, obviously they're...little...tiefs. Obviously.

Why was the Mind Flayer confused by the giant?

He couldn't wrap his head around it.

> ♟ **MIND FLAYERS AND FEEDING**
> Due to the unique feeding methodology of the Mind Flayer, they don't usually like to go after meals where leftovers will be prevalent. Have you ever tried brain that's been left for a week in the fridge? Not great.

What happened when the fighter discovered his bed was a mimic?

He hit the sack.

Did you hear about the hill giant
who ate six horses and a bunch of hay?

Don't worry, his condition is stable.

What's the most amorous monster of all?

The romanticore.

> **🎩 ROMANTIC MONSTERS**
> Honestly, this is a bit of a relief, since until this very moment, I had been laboring under the misapprehension that the most amorous monster was the aphrodisiorc, the memory of which still wakes me in cold sweats.

Did you hear about the chunky giant who wasn't very good?

He was a mediocre meaty ogre.

Why is a twelve-legged lizard monster with lightning breath a great friend?

It'll always behir for you.

What brand of underwear is preferred by fighters and paladins the world over?

Under Armour.

Did you hear about the cleric of a god who hated earth elementals?

He left no stone unturned.

What did the transmuter say when his girlfriend dumped him?

"I can change!"

What bear leads goblins into battle?

A bugbear.

What's a vampire's favorite
Coen brothers movie?

The Bloodsucker Proxy.

🎩 **A THEATRICAL CORRECTION**
Are you sure? Are you sure it isn't just *Blood Simple?*

A player asks his DM if he can change a few things on his sorceress character. The DM replies, "Okay, but this is the fifth time this month; do you think you might just prefer to make a new character?"

"Sure," replies the player, "but I think I'll make a guy this time."

"Why's that?"

"Well, I think sometimes I just re-spec women too much."

🎩 VIDEO GAMES

Dear me, a reference to video game terminology? I thought this was a collection of jokes about role-playing. Oh, very well, at least it is in reference to RPG video game terminology, but, Writer, you are on thin ice. A single reference to triple kills, or wave clearing at mid, and I shall quit my role as editor and comment smith, instanter!

Why was the wizard arrested for having a vial of Mind Flayer brain juice in his component pouch?

Trafficking in Illithid substances.

> 🧙 **ON WIZARD CRIMES**
> In the end, there was a brief period where the wizard thought he'd escaped the charges, but it turned out that he had misheard a call of "Hung abjurer."

Why is a dwarf less useful than a marble?

A marble detects a sloping surface
on any roll of a d6.

Why are there no vampire philosophers?

They don't reflect.

> ### 🦇 VAMPIRE PHILOSOPHY
> Several philosophers have, however, become vampires and mod-ified their teachings accordingly! Consider the vampire phrase "Cogito, ergo sum delectamenti," for example. "I think; therefore, I am delicious."

What do you call a weapon that does extra damage to garden implements?

A murder hoe bow.

Why did the human bard
only play for halflings?

He was big in the Shire.

Why do paladins prefer chain mail?

It's holey armor.

> ⚖ **PALADINS AND ARMOR**
> Honestly, with the state of those church-minded do-gooders in this day and age, I'm full well surprised the answer wasn't "They don't! The majority of them wear only collection plate."

Did you know that Beholders tend to have a large range of topics they know about?

It's because they're so well-rounded.

Why do vampires and liches speak in riddles?

They're cryptic.

🎩 A MATTER OF ENDLESS TIME

Indeed, that is true, but also consider that your average vampire is more than 300 years of age, and liches far older still. Then, consider living that long and still having to order your turkey club without mayo every day. An eternity of "Hold mayo; spicy pickles if you have them," stretching out before you like a gray hell. You'll begin to craft riddles as well.

Why is it unfair to play as a centaur?

They get more feats.

Why were planar beings always hanging out on the wizard's lawn?

His Gate wouldn't close.

🧙 WIZARDS AND THE HOA

Homeowners associations often find themselves butting heads with the resident wizard in his lofty tower. Grease all over the driveway, riotous Prismatic Walls everywhere when the list of acceptable colors reads, "Eggshell, ecru, or fanberry beige," and familiars exceeding the limits for appropriate pets in size, arcane might, and incorporeality. A few balrogs littering the lawn is invariably the last straw before fines are impudently taped to the tower doors.

What do you call a sorcerer who only uses Beam spells?

Ray.

> ### 🎩 AND AS FOR OTHER SORCERERS
> If you encounter a sorcerer who uses primarily illusion spells, you needn't ask for his name. You can just call him a dick.

Who should you call if you get locked out of your house?

A monk. They always have the ki.

> ### 🎩 ON FORGETTING YOUR KEYS
> I might have suggested contacting a rogue, the masters of picking locks, that are actually established in the lore, or a wizard, many of whom know the Knock spell to open locked doors, but no, no, your thing is fine as well. Carry on.

Why aren't Medusas good dates?

They objectify people.

Why are air elementals the best to do business with?

All the trade winds.

> 🔺 **AIR ELEMENTALS AND BUSINESS**
> That runs counter to what I've heard. Air elementals are good for
> a few tasks, but in matters of commerce, they blow.

ABOUT THE AUTHORS

Jon Taylor is a professional podcaster from San Diego. He has a degree in English Literature from UC Santa Cruz. He spent several years as a stand-up comic on the East Coast before moving back to Southern California. Jon is a cocreator and cohost of the *System Mastery* podcast with Jef, where they review and comment on odd classic RPGs, poking fun at obscure stories and systems while taking the game for a spin.

Jef Aldrich is also a professional podcaster from San Diego. Along with Jon he has spent the past five years building a podcast brand outside of the big network channels. Jef started entertaining people as a SeaWorld tour guide and eventually just started being funny for a living on his own. Jef is a cocreator and cohost of the *System Mastery* podcast with Jon.

Essential additions to
ANY PLAYER'S GAMING KIT!

PICK UP OR DOWNLOAD YOUR COPIES TODAY!